CRAFTS

Danielle Lowy and Katie Riley

QEB Publishing

Copyright © QEB Publishing 2014

First published in the United States by
QEB Publishing, Inc.
3 Wrigley, Suite A
Irvine, CA 92618

www.qed-publishing.co.uk

A CIP record for this book is available from the Library of Congress.

ISBN 978 1 60992 713 4

Printed in China

Designers: Martin Taylor and A Child
Editor: Ruth Symons
Copy editor: Catherine Saunders
Photography: Michael Wicks
Illustrators: Tom Connell and Barry Croucher
Editorial Director: Victoria Garrard
Art Director: Laura Roberts-Jensen
Models: Rio, Nana, Quinn, Vince, and Scarlett

Some children might be able to
do some or all of these projects
on their own, while others might need
more help. These are projects that you
can work on together, not only to avoid
any problems or accidents, but also to
share in the fun of making art.

At the top of the page for each project you will
find this handy key. It will tell you the level of
difficulty to expect from each project:

Quick creative fix

These projects are quick, easy, and perfect
for a beginner.

Sharpen your skills

Confident with your beginner skills?
Move onto these slightly tougher projects.

Ready for a challenge

For a challenging project you can really
get stuck into.

Creative masterpiece

Think you can tackle the toughest projects?
Try these out!

 Look out for this sign!
It means you will need
an adult to help you.

CONTENTS

Techniques 4
Festive Felt Garland 8
Christmas Sweater 10
Basket Advent Calendar 12
Star-Struck Clay Decorations 14
Paper Gift Bag 16
Ribbon Christmas Tree 18
Holly Candle Holder 20
Christmas Tree Card 22
Twirly Tinsel Decoration 24
3D Star Decoration 26
Sock Mouse 28
Mini Button Wreath 30
Lavender Hand Warmer 32
Snowflake Card 34
Jingle Bell Elf 36
Wrapping Paper 38
Candy Wreath 40
Paper Lantern 42
Paper Clip Ice Skate 44
Snow Globe 46
Paper Ornaments 48
Mitten Gift Tag 50
Button Tree 52
Angel Tree Topper 54
Festive Photo Props 56
Christmas Stocking 58
Snowball Scarf 60
Caroling Penguins 62
Index 64

TECHNIQUES

Some of the projects in this book require sewing and other simple techniques. If you need extra help, just refer to these pages!

THREADING

Use a single strand of thread for sewing thin fabrics. For thicker fabrics, or to make your stitches stronger, you can double the thread.

STITCHING

You will need to use stitches for some of the fabric-based projects in this book. You can also use them to add extra decoration to your projects.

Running Stitch
Sew up and down through the fabric. Make sure the stitches on both the top and the underside are the same size and in a straight line.

Single Threading
Pass the thread through the needle and tie a knot in one end.

Double Threading
Pass the thread through the needle. Make sure the needle is in the middle of the thread and knot both ends together.

Blanket Stitch
Push the needle through from back to front to make the first stitch. Start a second stitch next to it. Before you have pulled the thread all the way through, pull the needle through the looped thread from back to front. Repeat.

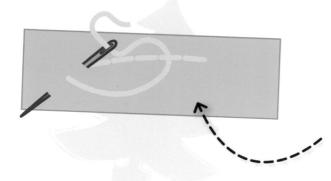

Back Stitch

Make a running stitch, then come up through the fabric a stitch ahead. Stitch backward to meet your first running stitch. Repeat in a neat line.

Whip Stitch

Place the two edges of the fabric you are joining close together. Sew stitches from one piece of fabric to the other to bind them tightly.

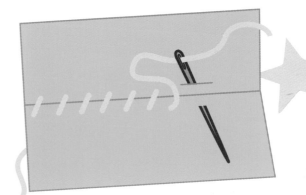

Chain Stitch

Pull the needle and thread from the back to the front of the cloth. Put the needle back into the point where it came up, and start to pull the thread back through. This will make a loop. While there is still a loop at the front of the material, bring the needle back up inside it. This will make the first chain. Repeat the action to make a row of chain stitches.

Satin Stitch

Mark out the shape you want and sew straight stitches closely together across the shape, taking care to keep the edges even.

KNOTS

Starting Knot

When sewing, it is important to tie a knot in the end of your thread. This will secure the tail of the thread at the back of your fabric.

2 Using your thumb, roll the thread off your finger.

3 Pull the loop toward the end of the thread to make a neat knot.

1 Wrap the thread around your index finger.

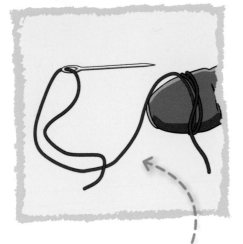

USING TEMPLATES

You can cut out the templates at the back of this book, or trace them onto paper, then cut them out.

To trace a template, put a piece of tracing paper over it and draw over the template in pencil. Turn the tracing paper over and draw over the lines again. Flip the tracing paper back to the right side and lay a sheet of paper beneath it. Shade over the tracing with your pencil to transfer the template.

Finishing Knot

To finish sewing, make a small stitch and sew through the loop before pulling it tight. Repeat to make two knots. Cut off the excess thread, leaving a small tail.

MAKE A POM-POM

Pom-poms are easy and fun to make. You can use a pom-pom to decorate any of the projects in this book!

YOU WILL NEED:
- Scissors
- Cardboard
- Yarn

1 Cut two identical doughnut rings from cardboard and place them together.

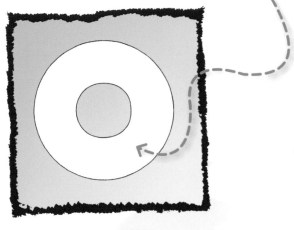

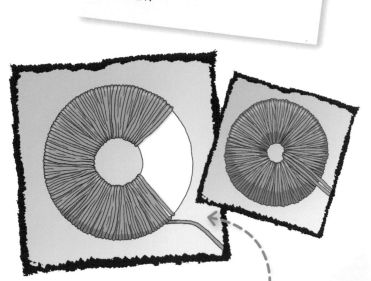

2 Wrap the yarn around the rings, going through the hole and around the outer edge. Keep wrapping until the hole in the middle is very tight.

3 Cut through the yarn around the edge of the rings, a layer at a time, until you meet the cardboard underneath.

4 Pass a length of yarn inbetween the two cardboard rings. Tie it tightly around all the yarn at the center. Now remove the cardbaord rings and reveal your pom-pom!

FESTIVE FELT GARLAND

Decorate your bedrooom with this festive garland.

YOU WILL NEED:

- Holly, ornament, stocking, and candy cane templates from the back of the book
- Red, green, and white felt
- Felt-tip pen
- Scissors
- Green and white embroidery thread
- Needle
- Small red and green buttons
- Ribbon
- Sequins

1 Cut out the garland templates at the back of the book.

2 Trace the shapes onto felt: green for holly leaves, white for the ornaments and the top of the stocking, and red for the stocking, the cane, and the holly berries. Cut them all out.

8

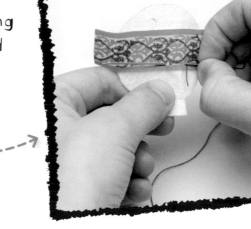

3 Decorate the ornaments by sewing on sequins or ribbons. Sew the red berries onto the holly and the tops onto the stockings using a running stitch (see page 4).

4 Sew on white stripes for the candy cane. Use one big stitch to make each stripe.

5 Thread 32 inches (80 cm) of green thread onto a needle. Sew the felt shapes onto the thread, adding buttons in between each shape. Sew an extra button onto the ornaments. Lastly, tie a loop at each end of the thread to hang it up by.

Try other shapes such as trees, snowmen, or stars and decorate them with stick-on gems.

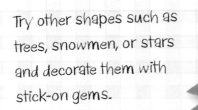

CHRISTMAS SWEATER

Make an old sweater festive and fabulous so you'll look and feel merry!

1 Cut out the reindeer templates at the back of the book. Using chalk, draw around the large template onto dark brown felt. Use the other template to draw two antlers onto light brown felt. Cut out the shapes.

2 Pin the face and antlers onto the middle of the sweater. Sew them on using a blanket stitch (see page 4).

3 Using the pom-pom instructions on page 7, make a red pom-pom about 2 inches (5 cm) wide. Sew it onto the reindeer's face with red yarn.

4 Glue the googly eyes above the nose using white glue. Let it dry.

5 Try on your new Christmas sweater and wow your friends and family!

Experiment with other designs such as a snowflake or this cheerful snowman.

BASKET ADVENT CALENDAR

This awesome advent calendar can be filled with gifts and used every year!

1 Fold a piece of red cardstock in half. Place the template onto the cardstock, with the bottom of the strips on the folded edge. Draw around the template and cut out the shape. Repeat this on the white cardstock.

2 Start by taking strip A through strip 1, then push strip 2 through strip A. Push strip A through strip 3, then strip 4 through strip A. Make sure you weave around and through the folds rather than over and under them.

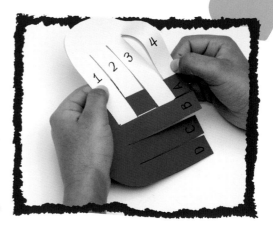

3 Weave each of the numbered strips through and around the lettered strips, as you did in step 2, until you have a checkered pattern.

4 Cut a 1 x 6 inch (2 x 15 cm) strip of red cardstock. Apply glue to each end of the strip and stick the ends inside the heart basket. Repeat steps 1 through 4 to make 24 heart baskets.

5 On a piece of A1 cardstock, draw a Christmas tree with four branches on each side. Cut it out and use it as a template to make a second tree shape.

6 Mark the middle point in both trees. Cut straight up from the bottom to the middle of one tree, and straight down from the top to the middle of the other. Slot the two trees together. Hang or pin your baskets to the branches of the tree.

STAR-STRUCK CLAY DECORATIONS

These decorations are simple to make but they have star quality!

YOU WILL NEED:

- Air dry clay, about 18 ounces (500 g)
- Rolling pin
- Star-shaped cookie cutter
- Drinking straw
- Baking paper
- Acrylic paint
- White glue watered down by ⅓ to be used as varnish
- Paintbrush
- Gold string
- Three mini beads

1 Roll some clay into a soft ball, about the size of a plum. Flatten the clay with a rolling pin until it is ¼ inch (5 mm) thick.

2 Press the cookie cutter into the clay to make a star shape. Smooth down any rough edges with your finger. Place the star on baking paper.

3 Make a hole in one of the points with the straw. Repeat steps 1 through 3 to make more stars or experiment with other cookie cutter shapes. Leave the shapes to dry for at least 24 hours.

14

4 Add a layer of paint to one side of the star. Let it dry, then add another layer. When that's dry, do the same on the other side. Paint the edges a different color. When the paint is dry, varnish the star with watered down glue and let it dry.

5 Thread the string through the hole, then thread on three mini beads. Tie the two ends of the string together to make a loop. Repeat with the other stars and hang up your decorations!

To make a textured star, press some lace or a doily into the clay in step 2. Remove the lace before leaving the clay to dry.

PAPER GIFT BAG

Use leftover wrapping paper to create your own gorgeous gift bags.

- Cardboard box
  (e.g. individual cereal box)
- Sheet of wrapping paper (big enough to wrap around the box with some extra)
- Pencil
- Ruler
- Scissors
- Glue stick
- Tape
- Hole punch
- 35 inch (90 cm) ribbon

1 Cut the paper so that it is $2\frac{1}{2}$ inches (6 cm) longer than the height of the box and can wrap around the box with a $1\frac{1}{2}$ inch (4 cm) overlap. Fold over the top $\frac{3}{4}$ inch (2 cm) and glue it down. This will give the top of your bag a neat edge.

2 Line up the top of the box with the top of the paper. Wrap the paper around the box and glue down the overlap.

3 Use the paper at the bottom of the box to make the base. Fold the top edge down, then fold in the left and right edges. Fold the bottom flap up and glue it down. Add tape for extra strength.

4 Make creases along all the folds of the paper and then gently remove the box. Carefully fold each side inwards and make a crease down the center.

5 Use a hole punch to make two holes on each side at the top of the bag. Cut the ribbon in half to use as handles. Thread each piece through two holes and knot it on the inside of the bag.

Check out teddy in his gift bag!

RIBBON CHRISTMAS TREE

This festive decoration will look great hanging from your tree. Try making several using different colored beads and ribbons.

YOU WILL NEED:

- 20 inches (50 cm) green ribbon
- 10 red beads ¼ inch (8 mm) wide
- 8 inches (20 cm) red thread or yarn
- Sewing needle (thin enough to fit through the beads)
- Scissors

1 Thread the needle and tie a big knot in the other end of the thread. Push a bead over the needle and pull it down to the knot. Take the needle around the side of the bead and pull it up through the bottom of the bead again.

2 Pull the needle and thread through the ribbon, about ³/₄ inch (2 cm) from one end. Pull the thread all the way through so that the ribbon sits on top of the bead.

3 Thread on another bead. Fold the ribbon over the second bead to make a loop about 1 ½ inches (3.5 cm) long. Hold the loop in place and take the needle and thread through the ribbon.

4 Keep adding beads, looping the ribbon back over each one. With each bead you add, make the loop slightly shorter. This will make a Christmas tree shape!

5 Thread on the last bead, then push the needle back through the top of it, leaving a short loop of thread. Holding the loop, take the needle around the side of the bead and down through the top again. Knot the thread and trim any loose ends.

"Oh Christmas tree! Oh Christmas tree!"

HOLLY CANDLE HOLDER

YOU WILL NEED:

- Clean jam jar with the labels removed
- Red and green tissue paper
- Black felt-tip pen
- Scissors
- Glue stick
- Glitter glue
- Battery night light or tea light candle

Help light Santa's way this Christmas with this twinkling candle holder.

1 Draw four holly leaves onto a sheet of green tissue paper. You can use one of the templates at the back of the book if you need help. Carefully cut out the shapes.

2 Apply some glue to the back of one holly leaf, then use your fingers to smooth it onto the jam jar. Glue on the rest of the leaves in the same way.

3 Draw four circular berries onto a sheet of red tissue paper. Cut them out and glue them between the holly leaves.

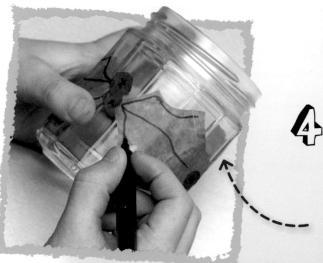

4 Using a black felt-tip pen, draw around the edge of each holly leaf. Then add a line down the center of each one. Make a small "x" in the middle of the red berries.

5 Wrap a piece of ribbon around the neck of the jam jar and cut it to size. Glue the ribbon in place.

Have a jolly holly Christmas!

Place a battery night light inside your jam jar or ask an adult to add a small tea light.

CHRISTMAS TREE CARD

A homemade Christmas card is so much nicer to receive than a store-bought one!

YOU WILL NEED:
- Christmas tree template from the back of the book
- Letter-sized white cardstock, folded in half
- Pencil
- Scissors
- Letter-sized sheet of green paper
- Brown and red paper
- Glue stick
- Tape
- Small piece of ribbon
- Stick-on gems
- Buttons
- 3 silver paper clips
- 4 colorful paper clips

1 Using the template, draw a tree on the inside of the folded cardstock (the left-hand side). Carefully use the point of the scissors to make a hole in the middle of the tree. Then cut out the tree shape, except for the trunk and pot.

2 Cut the sheet of green paper in half. Use the template to draw a tree shape on one half. Cut the other half into strips with straight, wavy, or zigzag edges. Make small cuts along the edges for a fringed effect.

3 Cut a ¹/₂ inch (1 cm) strip of brown paper. Glue it over the trunk on the green paper. Glue the green strips above the trunk, so that they overlap and cover the tree shape. Stick the green paper face down inside the white cardstock so it shows through.

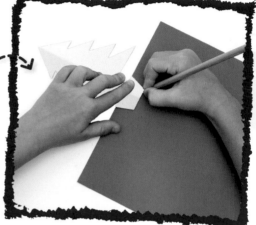

4 Use the template to draw the pot shape on the red paper. Using tape, stick a piece of ribbon to the back of the pot and tie it in a bow at the front. Glue the pot onto the front of the white cardstock.

5 Decorate the tree using sequins, buttons, stick-on gems, and paper clips. Make a star by crossing two paper clips and using a third to hold them in place. Glue it to the top of the tree.

Merry Christmas

TWIRLY TINSEL DECORATION

This simple decoration will jazz up your Christmas tree. Watch it sparkle as it twists and turns.

1 Fold the pipe cleaner over, about ¼ inch (0.5 cm) from one end and pinch it tight.

2 At the other end of the pipe cleaner, thread on a bead. Pull it as far as the folded end.

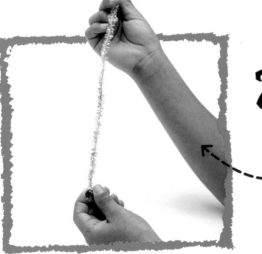

3 Add more beads, leaving a ½ inch (1.5 cm) gap between each one. Leave a gap of 1 inch (2.5 cm) at the top of the pipe cleaner.

4 To create the twist, hold the folded end of the pipe cleaner between your thumb and first finger. Using your other hand, twist the pipe cleaner around your finger.

5 Fold the thread in half and knot the two loose ends together. Place the top of the pipe cleaner through the loop of thread, fold it over, and squeeze it closed.

You can now hang your decoration from your tree or in a window.

3D STAR DECORATION

This **3D decoration** can be folded flat after **Christmas** and stored away for next year.

1 Cut out the template from the back of the book and draw around it five times onto the back of the wrapping paper. These will be the five points that join together to make the star. Cut out the shapes and draw dashed lines between the points, as shown on the template.

2 Fold along the dashed lines, using a ruler to keep your folds neat. Make a ½ inch (1 cm) cut at the joint between the two pointed tips of the shape.

3 Glue along the long tab down one side of the shape. Stick it to the long side facing it to make one point of the star. Do this with the other four points.

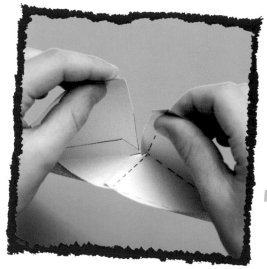

4 Glue two points together using the short tabs. Keep adding points until all five are glued together with one opening left.

5 Fold the thread in half and thread it onto a needle, as shown below. Push the needle through the paper fold 3/4 inch (2 cm) from the opening and pull it up on the opposite side. Take the needle through the looped thread, and pull it firmly.

Thread the needle like this.

SOCK MOUSE

Give an old sock a **Christmas** makeover. It makes a great gift or an unusual decoration!

YOU WILL NEED:

- Mouse templates from the back of the book
- Old sock
- Paper and pencil
- Scissors
- Small handful of stuffing
- Uncooked rice, about ¼ cup (70 g)
- A pinch of dried lavender
- Needle and thread
- Funnel or paper to make a cone.
- 3 tiny buttons (2 matching)
- Felt scraps

1 Cut out the body template and pin it to the edge of the sock. Cut along the rounded edge of the template, through both layers of fabric.

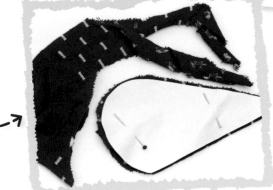

2 Turn the material inside out. Starting at the pointy end, sew up the side using a back stitch (see page 5). Leave an opening at the bottom and turn the sock the right way out.

3 Fill about 1 inch (2.5 cm) of the pointy end with stuffing. Use a funnel or make a paper cone to fill the mouse with the rice and lavender. Fold in the cloth at the bottom and sew up using a whip stitch (see page 5).

4 Using the templates, cut a tail and ears out of felt. Sew them onto the mouse using a whip stitch.

5 Sew a button onto the end of the nose and two buttons on for eyes.

"Mmm, smells nice!"

I just can't wait 'til Christmas!

You could give your mouse a fairy wand or halo made from tinsel pipe cleaners. Why not make several mice for a cute nativity scene?

MINI BUTTON WREATH

YOU WILL NEED:

- 10 large buttons about ¾–1 inch (20-25 mm) wide
- 10 small to medium buttons about ¼–½ inch (10-15) mm wide
- 20 inches (50 cm) jewelry wire (18 ga thickness works well)
- Ruler
- Strong scissors (to cut wire)
- Ribbon (optional)

Add some color to your tree or your bedroom with this cute-as-a-button wreath.

1 Put 10 large buttons in a circle and place the smaller buttons on top of them.

2 Loosely bend the wire in half to mark a halfway point. Thread one end of the wire through the back of a large button, then a small button. Pull the wire through to the halfway point.

3 Then thread the wire back through the front of both buttons. If a button has four holes, thread it diagonally through two of them.

4 Thread the wire through another pair of buttons in the same way. Keep going until there are five pairs of buttons on one side of the wire. Then thread five pairs onto the other side.

5 Bend the wire into a circle and twist the two ends together. Use the spare wire to make a loop to hang your wreath up with.

For a finishing touch, add a pretty ribbon.

LAVENDER HAND WARMER

This scented hand warmer is perfect for cold winter mornings. Heat it up before going out, then pop it in your pocket.

- Mug
- White felt
- Pen
- Scissors
- Embroidery needle
- Black, orange, and green embroidery thread
- Pins
- Small amount of black and green felt
- Small pom-pom
- Uncooked rice, about ¼ cup (70 g)
- Dried lavender (2 teaspoons)
- Funnel or paper for cone
  Note: Do not use metallic threads or materials as they are not microwaveable.

1 Using a pen, draw around the mug to make two circles on the white felt. Cut out the circles.

2 Draw a face onto one of the circles. Embroider over the outline using a back stitch for the mouth and a satin stitch for the eyes and nose (see page 5).

3 Pin the two circles together with the embroidered side face up. Starting above one eye, sew a blanket stitch (see page **4**) around the circles. Finish above the other eye, leaving a gap for stuffing.

4 Use a funnel or make a paper cone to fill the snowman with rice and lavender. Sew up the gap using a blanket stitch.

5 Draw around the curve of the mug to make the hat shape. Cut a strip of felt for the border. Use a back stitch to sew them both to the front of the snowman, then stitch on a pom-pom.

Make any shape you like!

Heat the hand warmer in a microwave for 20 to 30 seconds. Ask an adult for help, if you need it.

SNOWFLAKE CARD

Create custom-made festive cards using simple beaded snowflake patterns. Each card can have a unique design!

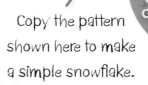

Copy the pattern shown here to make a simple snowflake.

1 Starting in the center of the pegboard, arrange the beads into a snowflake pattern.

2 Place the greaseproof paper over the pegboard and ask an adult to help you move a hot iron over it for about 30 seconds or until the beads have fused together.

3 Wait about five minutes for the paper and snowflake to cool, then peel the greaseproof paper away from the snowflake. Follow steps 1 through 3 to make two smaller snowflakes.

4 Fold the letter-sized cardstock in half and arrange the snowflakes on the front. When you are happy with the design, apply a thin layer of glue to the back of each snowflake and stick them in place.

5 Write a festive greeting on the front of the card using a felt-tip pen.

Merry Christmas

NOEL

SEASON'S GREETINGS

JINGLE BELL ELF

Collect pine cones in autumn—or buy them in a craft store—and make this funny little decoration.

- Elf hat template from the back of the book
- Small wooden ball
- Pine cone
- Red felt
- White felt
- Scissors
- Strong red thread
- Needle
- Small craft bell
- White glue
- Black felt-tip pen
- Red felt-tip pen

1 Dab some glue onto the ball and the top of the pine cone. Wait for a few seconds until the glue is tacky, and then put the ball on top of the pine cone. Hold it in place for a few minutes while the glue dries.

2 Draw around the hat template onto the red felt and cut it out. Put a line of white glue along one straight edge, wrap it around to form a cone shape, and stick it down. Add some glue around the inside of the hat and stick it onto the wooden ball.

3 Cut a strip of red felt and a strip of white felt, each about 3 x 1/2 inch (7 x 0.5 cm). Dab white glue onto the red felt and wrap it between the pine cone and the wooden ball to make a scarf. Glue the white felt to the bottom of the hat.

"Jingle bells, jingle bells, jingle all the way..."

4 Thread the needle and pull it through the tip of the hat, from back to front, leaving **4** inches (10 cm) of thread at the back. Thread on the craft bell. Remove the needle and tie the two ends of the thread together to form a loop.

5 Using felt-tip pens, draw a face onto the wooden ball. Finally, hang your elf from your Christmas tree, or dangle it anywhere you choose!

WRAPPING PAPER

Make your gifts look too good to open with this pretty wrapping paper.

- Christmas tree template from the back of the book
- Pen
- Sponge cloth
- Scissors
- Medium cardboard roll
- White glue
- Colored paint
- Paintbrush
- Large sheet of colored paper
- Gold star sequins or stickers

1 Using a pen, draw around the Christmas tree template onto sponge cloth twice. Carefully cut out the shapes.

2 Glue the foam tree shapes onto the cardboard roll with white glue. Leave them to dry.

3 Using a paintbrush, gently paint the Christmas tree with colored paint. This is your stamp.

4 Starting from the outside edge, roll the stamp across the sheet of paper toward you. Add more paint to the stamp as necessary, and continue rolling.

5 Leave the paper to dry and then decorate it with sequins or stickers.

If you want to use the stamp again, wrap it in plastic wrap to stop the sponge from drying out.

CANDY WREATH

Hang this wreath on your door so Santa can help himself to a candy!

- Wire coat hanger
- 2 long pipe cleaners, about 24 inches (60 cm) long
- 40–50 wrapped candies
- Elastic thread or other strong thread
- Scissors
- 5-6 yards (meters) red, green, and gold ribbon
- 24 inches (60 cm) gold ribbon

1 Pull the wire hanger to make a hoop shape.

2 Twist the pipe cleaners around the hook at the top of the hoop.

3 Cut 3 inches (8 cm) of elastic thread and tie it around one end of a candy. Use the same thread to tie the candy to the hoop, making two knots. Tie all the candies around the hoop in the same way.

4 Cut the ribbons into 6 inch (15 cm) pieces. Tie them in bows between the candies, mixing the colors as you go. Do this until the hoop is full.

5 Tie the gold ribbon in a bow at the top of the hoop. Now hang up your wreath. To take a candy, just undo the wrapper!

Friends and family will love this sweet idea!

As an extra special wreath, cut and sew a small felt bag to hang inside your wreath. Fill it with chocolate coins for an extra treat at the door!

PAPER LANTERN

These paper lanterns are fun to make and will add a festive touch to your home. Make them in any color you want!

1 Use a pencil and ruler to mark the letter-sized cardstock at 1 inch (2.5 cm) spaces along both long sides. Join the marks to make 10 straight pencil lines. Cut off the large section at the end and put it aside.

2 Fold the cardstock in half lengthways. Draw a ³/₄ inch (2 cm) wide pencil margin on both sides of the open edge. Starting at the folded edge, cut along the horizontal pencil lines until you reach the margin.

3 Unfold the card and lay it flat with the pencil lines facing up. Apply a line of glue along the strip on the far right. Carefully curl the card to make a cylinder and press firmly to stick the sides together.

4 Cut a 1 inch (2.5 cm) strip from the cardstock you set aside in step 1. Apply glue to each end of the strip and stick the ends to the inside of the lantern to make a handle. Glue the gold ribbon around the top of the lantern.

5 Using the star template, draw star shapes onto colored cardstock. Cut out the stars and glue them to the lantern.

Make several lanterns and hang them on a piece of thread to create a garland.

PAPER CLIP ICE SKATE

Add a touch of winter glamor to your Christmas tree with these cute mini ice skates.

YOU WILL NEED:

- Ice skate template from the back of the book
- Green felt
- Scissors
- A 2 inch (5 cm) paper clip
- Green thread
- Needle
- 5 inches (12 cm) length of ¼ inch (3 mm) green ribbon
- 2 X 1 inch (2.5 cm) lengths of ¼ inch (3 mm) green ribbon
- 4 green sequins
- White glue
- Felt-tip pen

1 Cut out the template and place it onto the green felt. Draw around it using a felt-tip pen and cut out the shape.

2 Pull the felt shape halfway through the paper clip. Fold the long strip of ribbon in half and dab a little glue on the ends. Glue the ribbon inside the top left corner of the skate and press the felt halves together.

44

3 Starting at the toe of the ice skate, sew the two halves together using a blanket stitch (see page 4). Make sure that you stitch through the end of the ribbon loop to secure it in place.

4 Apply a little glue to the back of the two short lengths of ribbon. Stick one around the front of the ice skate, about ½ inch (1 cm) from the top. Stick the other piece just below it.

5 Using white glue, stick sequins over the ribbon ends to look like buttons.

These look very "ice" on the tree!

SNOW GLOBE

Make sure it's a white Christmas with a homemade snow globe.

- Oven bake clay in white, black, and orange
- Green felt
- Scissors
- Clean jam jar and lid
- Water
- Glycerine (available from most craft stores)
- Strong multipurpose glue
- White glitter
- Christmas ribbon

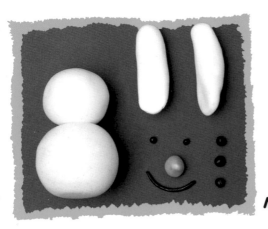

1 Use white clay to make a snowman's head, body, and arms. Use black clay to make buttons, eyes, and a mouth. Use orange clay to make a nose. Then assemble your snowman.

2 Make a small cube with black clay and pinch out the bottom to create a hat. Put the hat on your snowman. Ask an adult to bake it in the oven, following the instructions on the pack.

3 When the snowman has cooled, cut a narrow strip of felt and tie it on. You can dab a little glue around the neck to make sure the scarf stays put.

4 Glue your snowman to the inside of the jam jar lid. Leave it to dry. Wrap the ribbon around the edge of the lid and cut it to fit. Glue the ribbon in place.

5 Add water to the jar until it is nearly full, then fill it to the top with glycerine. Add the glitter and stir the mixture. Screw the lid on tightly and shake your snow globe to create a glittering snowstorm.

"Let it snow, let it snow..."

If you don't have time to make a snowman, you could use a pretty cake topper instead and just follow steps 4 and 5.

PAPER ORNAMENTS

Use colored paper or reuse leftover wrapping paper to make a pretty ornament.

1 Use the cup to draw 12 circles onto the patterned paper and 12 onto the plain paper.

2 Cut out all of the circles. Glue the back of the plain circles to the back of the patterned circles. You will now have 12 circles in total.

3 Fold each circle in half, then open it up again. Stack the circles, alternating plain side up and patterned side up.

4 Staple in the fold to fix the 12 circles together. Tie a piece of ribbon along the fold and knot it at the top.

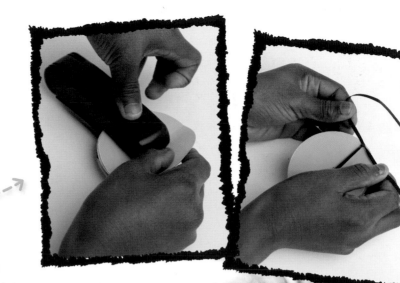

5 Place a glue dot on the bottom right of one circle and glue it to the facing flap. Turn over to the next circle. Place a glue dot to the top right of the circle and glue it to the facing flap. Alternate high and low glue dots until all of the flaps are stuck together.

For a simpler craft, use double-sided paper. Cut out 12 circles and skip step 2.

49

MITTEN GIFT TAG

Give your presents a pretty personal touch with this mitten-shaped gift tag.

- Templates from the back of the book
- Red cardstock
- White cardstock
- Patterned cardstock
- Pencil
- Scissors
- Glue stick
- Ruler
- 8 inch (20 cm) ribbon
- Hole punch
- Red or white string

1 Draw around the mitten template onto the red cardstock and cut out the shape. Draw around the template onto the white cardstock, adding a frilly edge, then cut out the shape. Glue the red mitten to the white mitten.

2 Draw 16 diamonds onto the white cardstock, using the template, and cut them out. Arrange eight diamonds into a snowflake and glue them onto the top of the mitten. Use the remaining diamonds to make a second snowflake.

3 Draw around the trim template onto the patterned cardstock. Cut out the shape. Glue the trim onto the base of the mitten.

4 Cut a triangle out of each end of the ribbon. Create a bow by looping half of the ribbon forward, and the other half backward. Glue the ribbon together in the middle, and stick it to the base of the mitten.

5 Use a hole punch to make a hole in the thumb of the mitten. Pull the string halfway through the hole and knot the two ends together to make a loop. Write a personal message on your gift tag.

BUTTON TREE

These cute decorations will look lovely dangling from your Christmas tree.

- 3 small brown buttons
- A selection of 8-10 different-sized green buttons
- Star-shaped button
- Fishing wire or clear thread
- Red ribbon
- Stick-on gems

1 Stack the three brown buttons. Then stack the green buttons, with the largest at the bottom and smallest at the top.

2 Fold the fishing wire in half to make a loop. Thread on the three brown buttons, taking each end of wire through one of the holes in each button. The buttons should now sit at the bottom of the loop.

3 Thread on the green buttons, starting with the largest and finishing with the smallest.

4 Thread on the star button. Knot the end of the wire and then tie it to a loop of ribbon.

5 Add some stick-on gems to decorate your tree.

A little tree for a big tree!

A button tree also makes a festive key ring charm. What a great gift!

ANGEL TREE TOPPER

Give a basic ornament a heavenly makeover with some wire and beads. It's tree-mendous!

- Small plastic ornament, approximately 12 inches (300 mm) in circumference
- 32 inches (80 cm) of wire for body (18 ga)
- 20 inches (50 cm) of extra thin wire for wings (25 ga)
- At least 150 seed beads and about 50 other small beads
- 6 x 8 inch (15 x 20 cm) piece of white tissue paper
- White glue and paddle
- Lump of modeling clay or adhesive putty
- Scissors
- Small pliers (optional)

1 Thread the long wire about 2 inches (5 cm) through the loop on the ornament. Wind the wire tightly around the neck of the ornament.

2 Thread the beads onto the other end of the wire, mixing sizes and colors. About ³/₄ inch (2 cm) before the end, loop the wire back on itself, using your fingers or small pliers.

3 Hold the ornament down on the table and coil the wire around it into a flat spiral. Then carefully pull the spiral downwards to make a cone shape.

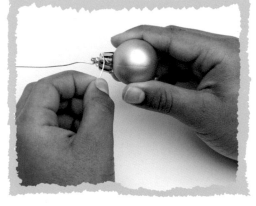

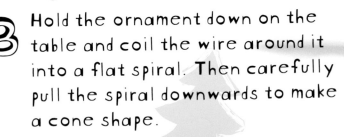

4 Bend the thin wire into a circle and twist the ends together, leaving two 2¼ inch (6 cm) tails. Pull the top of the circle down to the tails. This will make two wings. Wind the end of the wire around the join to secure the shape.

5 Spread a thin layer of glue onto the tissue paper. Place the wings at one edge, with the tails sticking out, and fold the paper over. Stand the wire tails in modeling clay and leave the wings to dry overnight.

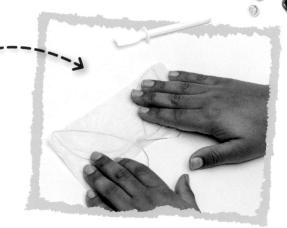

6 Trim the dry tissue paper around the edge of the wings. Fix them to the ornament by twisting the wire tails around its neck.

Your Christmas tree looks angelic!

FESTIVE PHOTO PROPS

Take some hilarious Santa selfies with these fun photo props. You'll have a very merry time!

1 Choose the shapes for your photo props from the templates at the back of the book. Cut out the shapes or trace them onto white paper and cut them out.

2 Draw around the shapes onto colored cardstock. If you're making the Santa hat, draw around the whole shape onto the red cardstock. Then cut out the bobble and fur trim from the template and draw them onto the white cardstock.

3 Carefully cut out the shapes. You can use other templates to add details such as holly to decorate your props.

4 Glue details, such as a fur trim or glitter, onto your main prop. For Santa, you could stick cotton pads onto your white cardstock.

5 Fix a kebab stick to the back of each shape using strong tape. Now hold up the props and say "cheese!"

"Cheese!"

"Ho ho ho!"

CHRISTMAS STOCKING

Hang up this fleece stocking and see what surprises appear inside it on Christmas Day!

1 Cut out or trace the template and pin it onto one piece of red fleece. Draw around it with chalk and cut out the shape. Repeat to make the other half of the stocking.

2 Cut the heel off the paper template, pin it onto the green fleece, draw around it, and cut it out. Glue it to the front of the stocking.

3 Cut the zigzag border off the top of the paper template. Pin it to the green fleece, draw around it, and cut it out. Sew a pom-pom onto every point. Glue the fleece to the front of the stocking.

4 Glue on ribbon strips to decorate the stocking and leave it to dry.

5 Pin the two sides of the stocking together. Sew around the edge using a blanket stitch (see page 4), leaving the top of the stocking open. Sew the bell to the end of the toe.

Look! Santa's been here!

SNOWBALL SCARF

This special scarf is sure to keep you warm through the winter!

- Thin cardboard
- Compass
- Pencil
- Scissors
- White yarn
- Silver or sparkly yarn
- Tape
- 1½ yards (1.5 m) strong thread

1 Using a pencil and compass, draw a circle 3 inches (7 cm) wide onto cardboard. Draw a ³/₄ inch (2 cm) wide circle inside it. Cut out the ring shape. Use this shape to draw and cut out another cardboard ring.

2 Gather three 1 yard (1 m) lengths of yarn and wrap a piece of tape around them at one end. Place your two cardboard rings together and wrap the yarn around them, pulling them by the tape.

3 Keep wrapping until the ring is covered and the hole in the middle is very tight. Use more yarn if you need to.

4 Cut through the yarn around the edge of the ring. Slide a 4 inch (10 cm) length of yarn between the two rings. Wrap it twice around the yarn at the center and tie it tightly. Gently remove the cardboard rings.

5 Make another 20 pom-poms, in a mix of white and sparkly yarn. Tie the last pom-pom together with one end of the long thread. Using a needle, pull the thread through the middle of the next pom-pom, loop it back around, and pull it through the pom-pom again. Thread each pom-pom twice in this way until you reach the end.

A great gift for Mom!

CAROLING PENGUINS

Make this caroling penguin with a cute bobble hat!

1 Paint the cardboard tube black and leave it to dry. Draw around the body template onto white felt. Cut it out and glue it onto the tube. Add the two googly eyes, about 1 inch (2.5 cm) from the top of the tube.

2 Using the template, draw two feet and a beak onto the orange felt. Then draw around the arm template twice onto the black felt. Cut out all the shapes. Put the arms to one side.

3 Dab glue onto the end of the feet and stick them to the inside of the tube. Fold the beak in half and stick it below the eyes.

4 Cut out the sheet music template and fold it in half. Glue one felt arm to each side of the sheet music and then stick the arms to the body.

5 To make the hat, cut off the top of an old sock. Tie the yarn tightly around the cut edge and glue the fluffy ball on top. Put the hat on the penguin.

"We wish you a merry Christmas!"

You could make a group of penguins to sing together. Why not give some of them scarves, or even earmuffs?

INDEX

back stitch 5

beads
 angel tree topper 54–55
 ribbon Christmas tree 18–19
 snowflake card 34–35
 twirly tinsel decoration 24–25

blanket stitch 4

buttons
 button tree 52–53
 mini button wreath 30–31

card
 basket advent calendar 12–13
 caroling penguins 62–63
 Christmas tree card 22–23
 festive photo props 56–57
 mitten gift tag 50–51
 paper gift bag 16–17
 paper lantern 42–43
 snowflake card 34–35

chain stitch 5

clay
 snow globe 46–47
 star-struck clay decorations 14–15

felt
 Christmas sweater 10–11
 festive felt garland 8–9
 jingle bell elf 36–37
 lavender hand warmer 32–33
 paper clip ice skate 44–45

jars
 holly candle holder 20–21
 snow globe 46–47

knots 6

paper
 3D star decoration 26–27
 Christmas tree card 22–23
 paper clip ice skate 44–45
 paper gift bag 16–17
 paper ornaments 48–49
 photo props, festive 56–57
 wrapping paper 38–39

pom-poms 7
 snowball scarf 60–61

running stitch 4

satin stitch 5

socks
 caroling penguins 62–63
 sock mouse 28–29

stitches 4–5

templates 6

threading 4

tree decorations
 angel tree topper 54–55
 button tree 52–53
 jingle bell elf 36–37
 mini button wreath 30–31
 paper clip ice skate 44–45
 paper ornaments 48–49
 ribbon Christmas tree 18–19
 star-struck clay decorations 14–15
 twirly tinsel decoration 24–25

whip stitch 5

wreath
 candy wreath 40–41
 mini button wreath 30–31